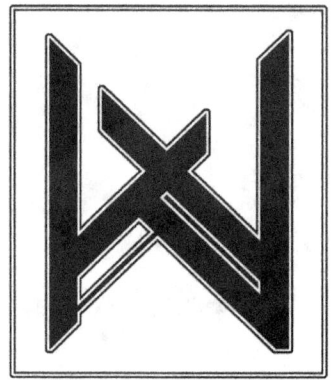

First Printing

www.dwaynewingert.com

The Color of Myth & Magic
Coloring Book
by
D Wingert

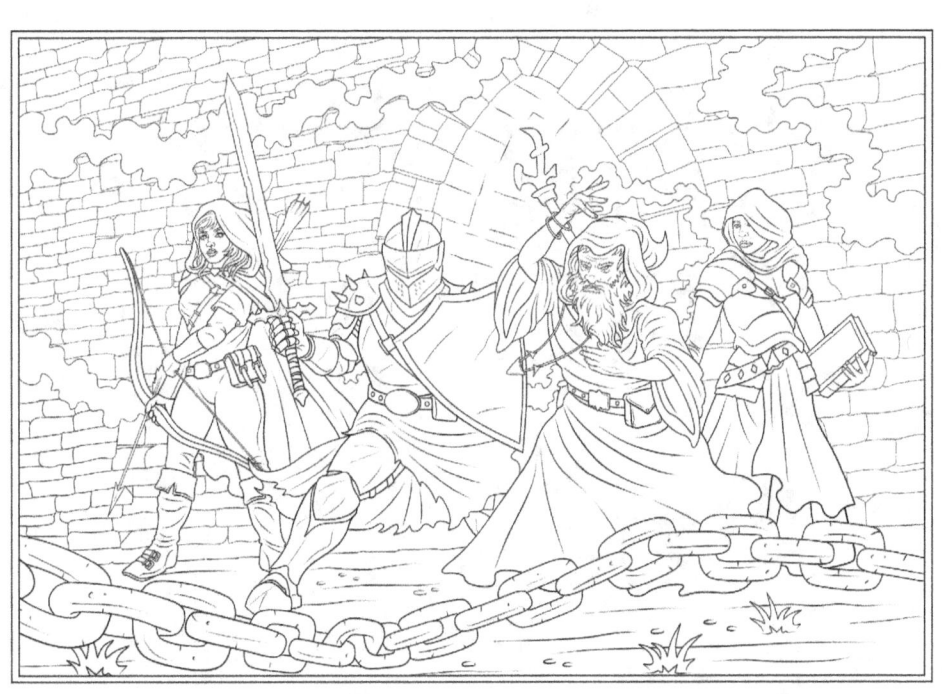

Dragon

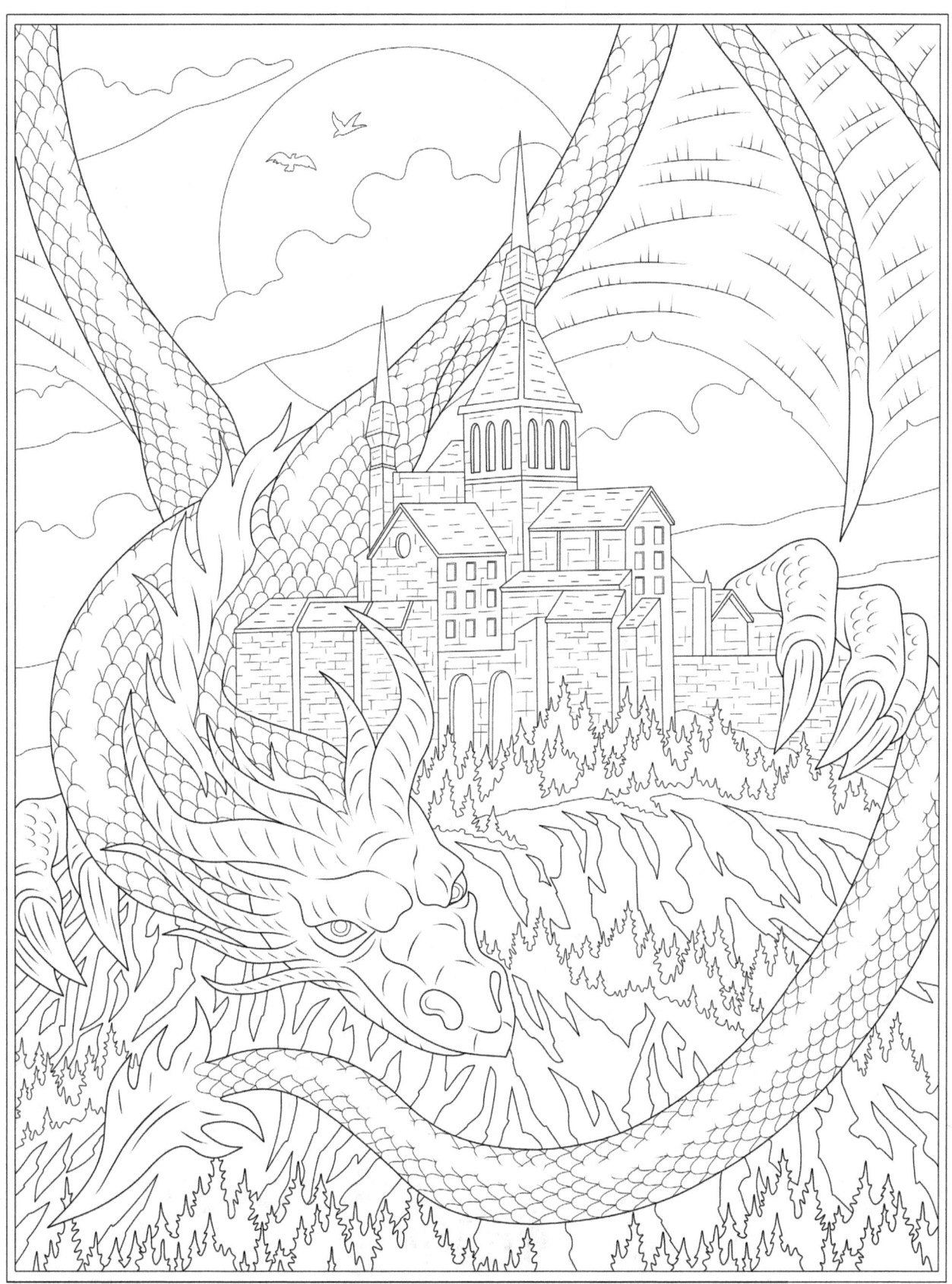

Wizard

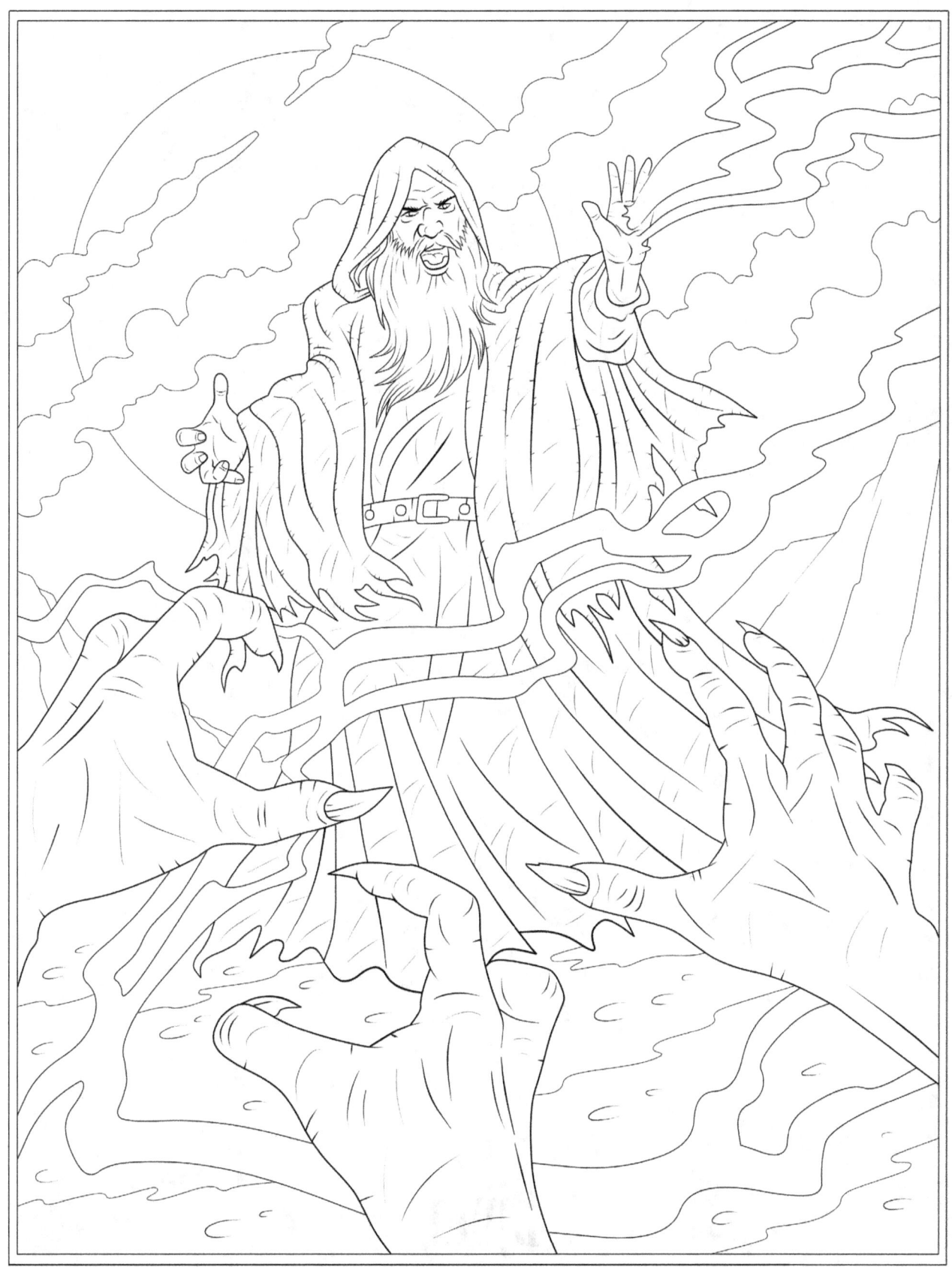

Djinn

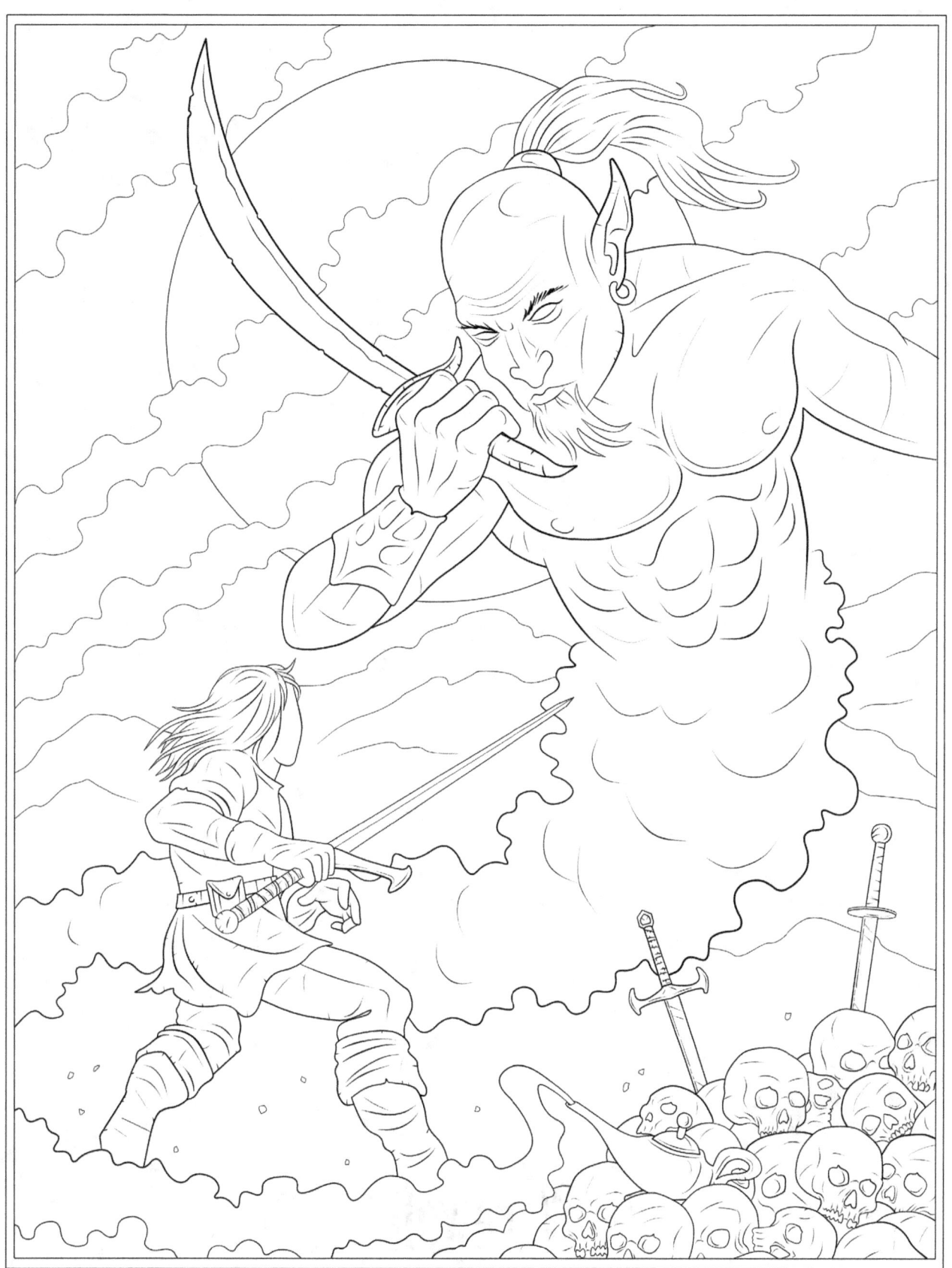

Werewolf

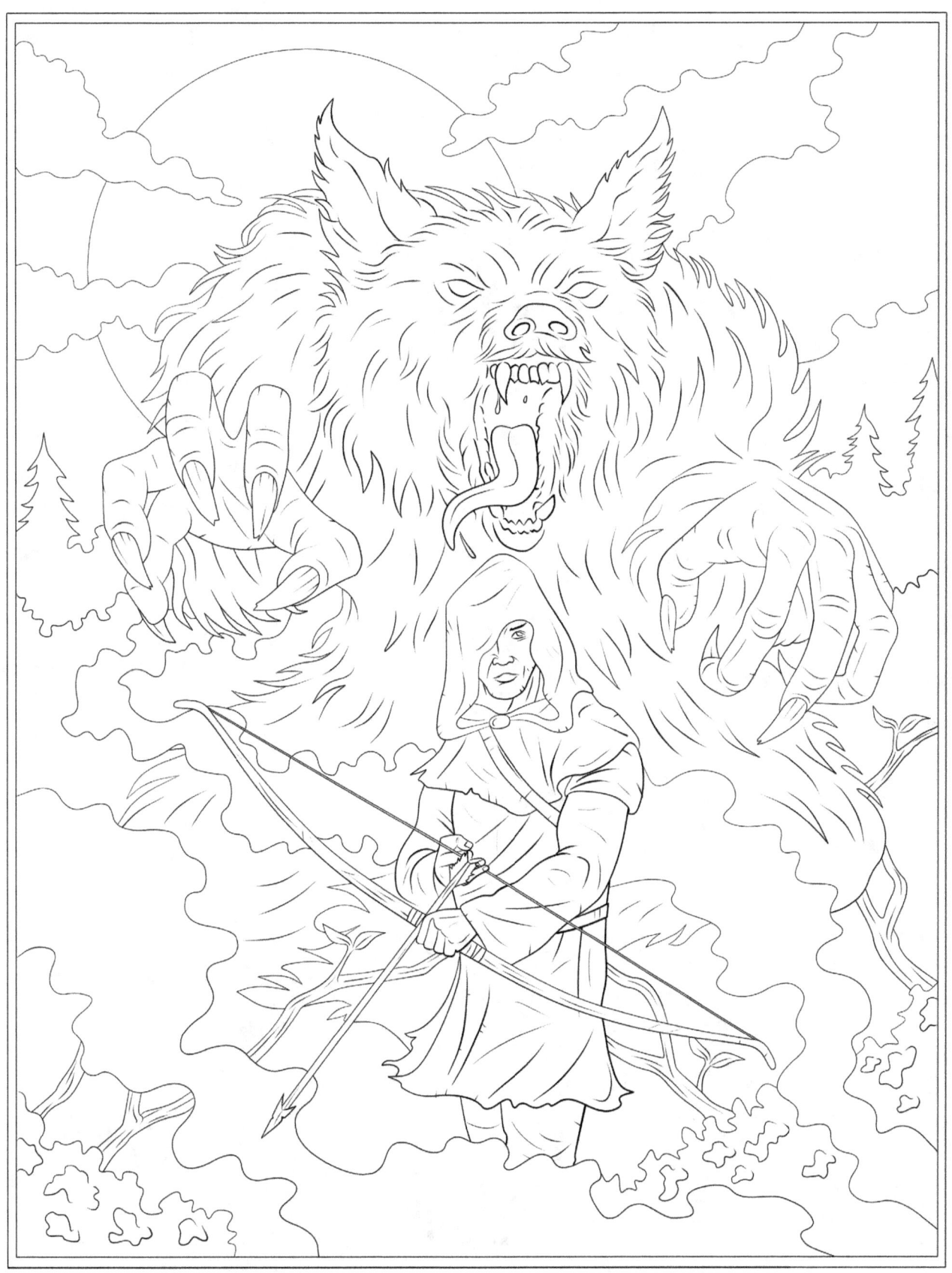

Cyclops

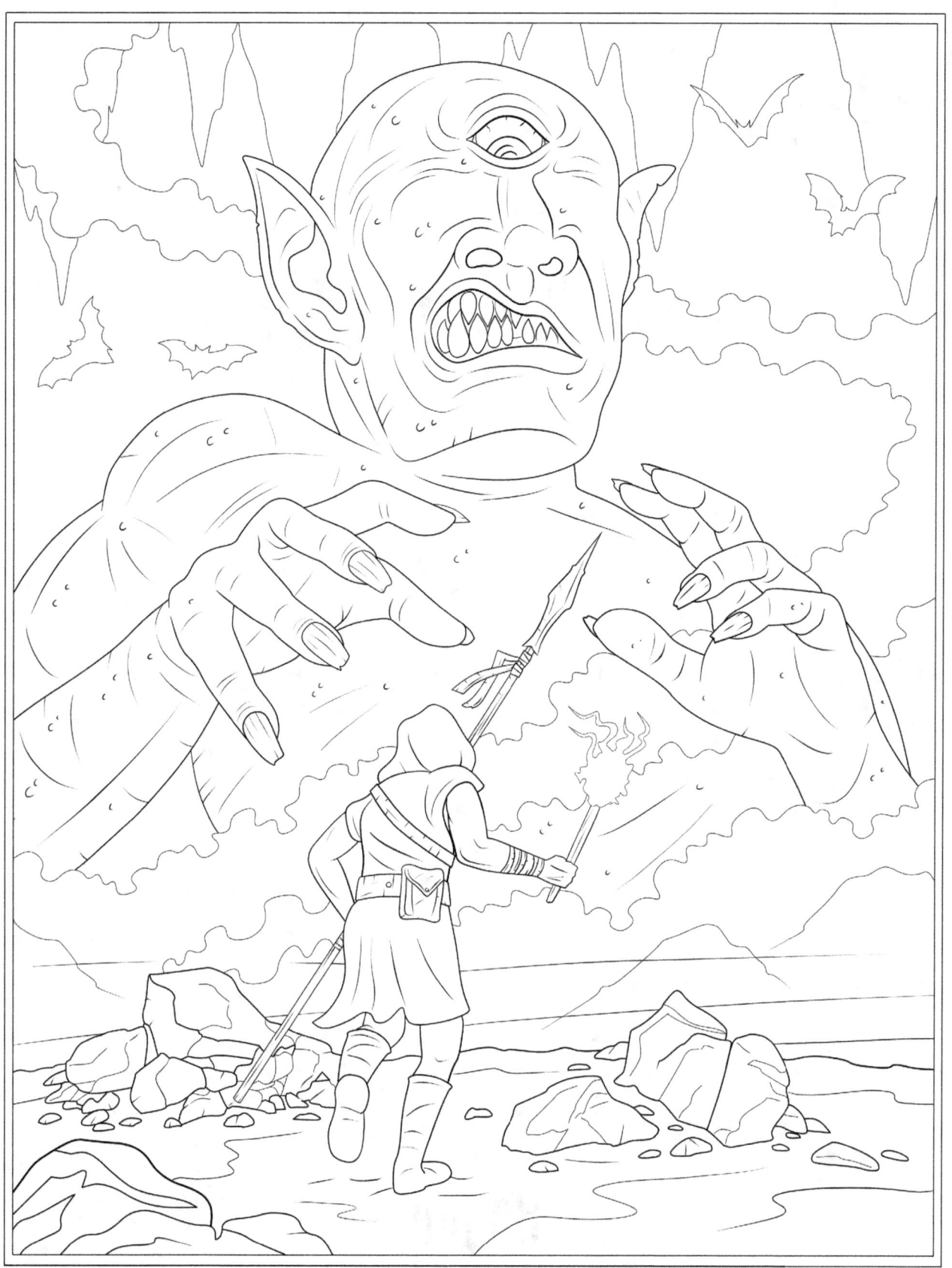

Rogue

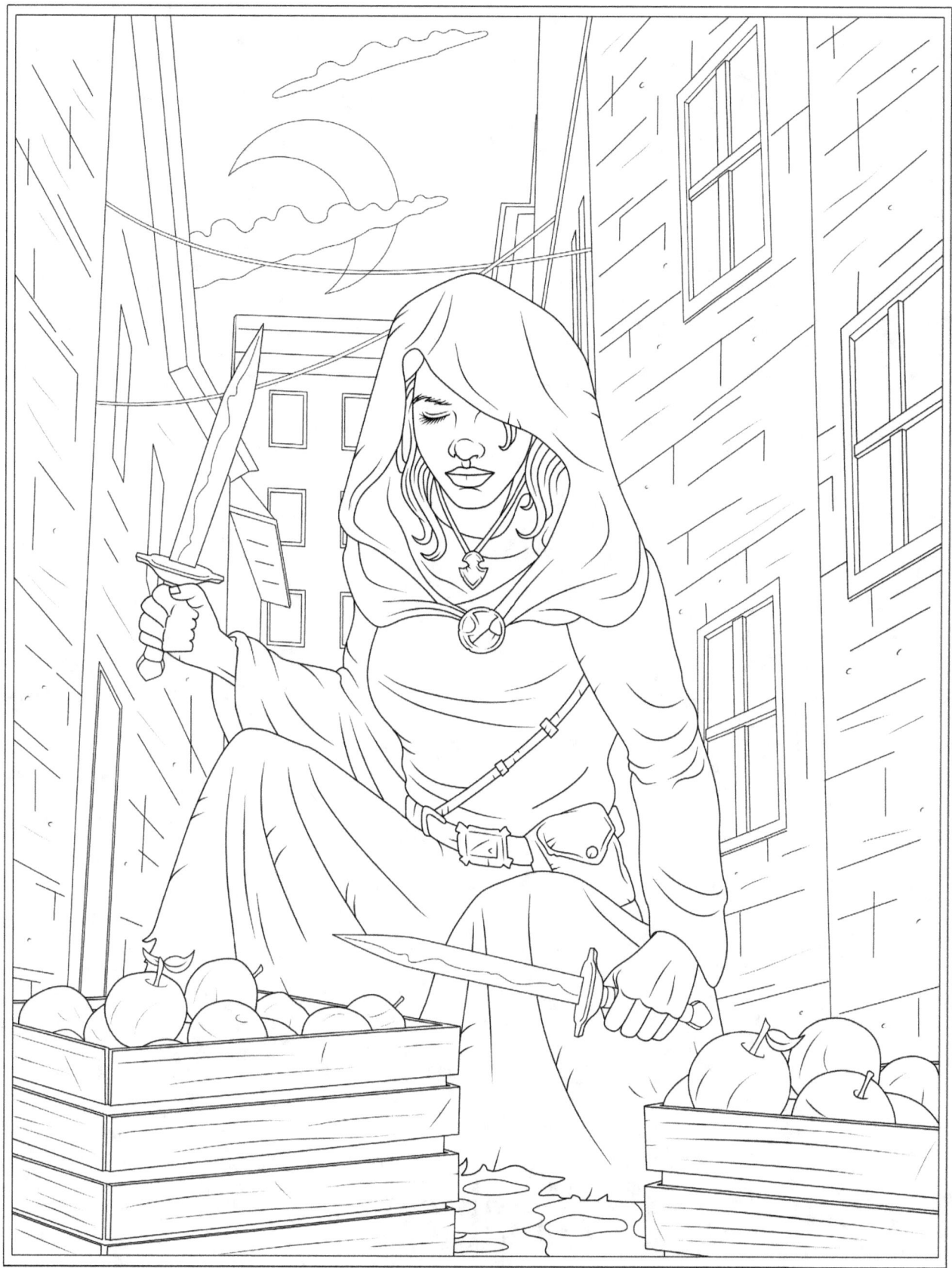

Zombies

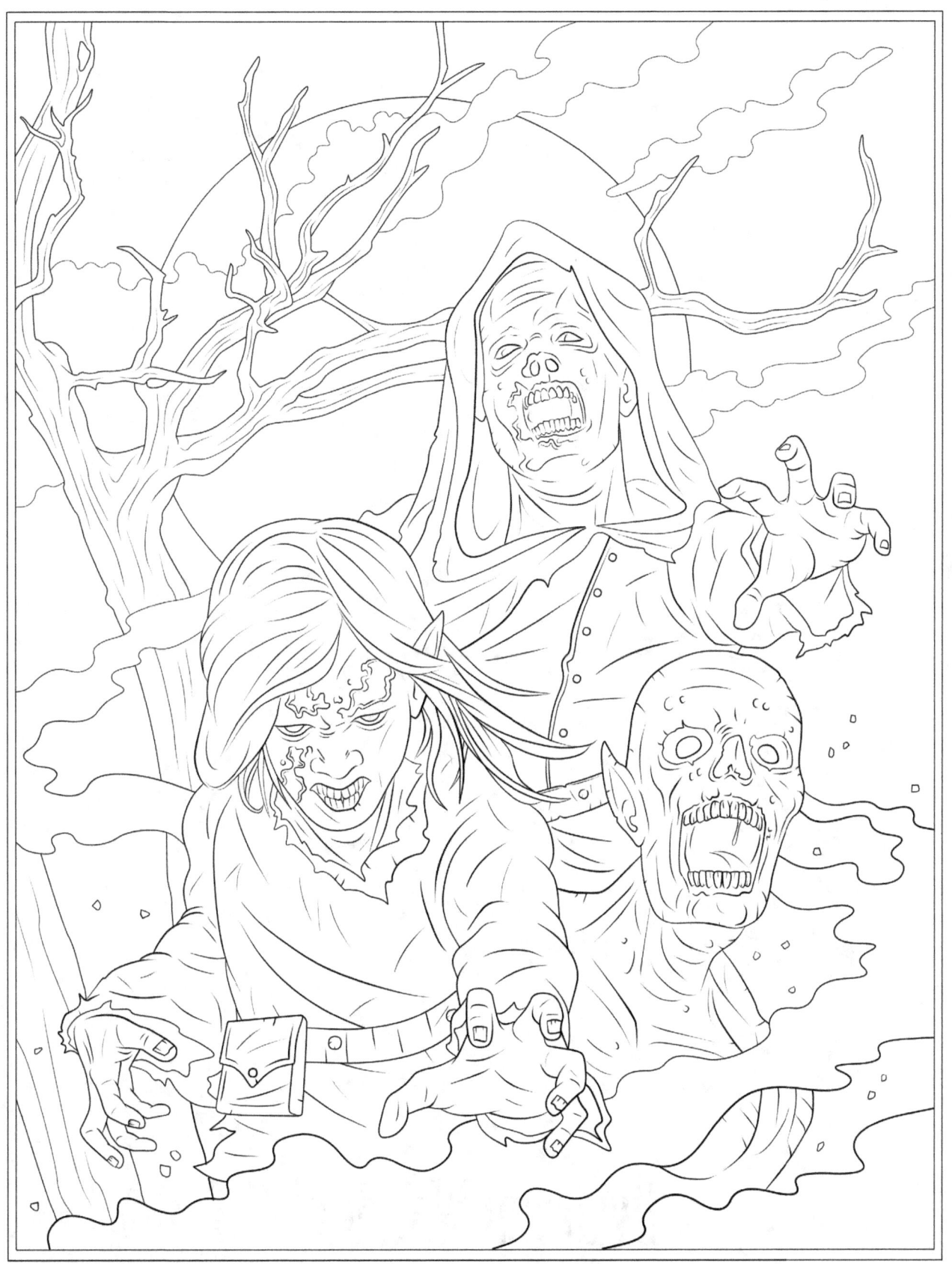

Dwarven Warrior

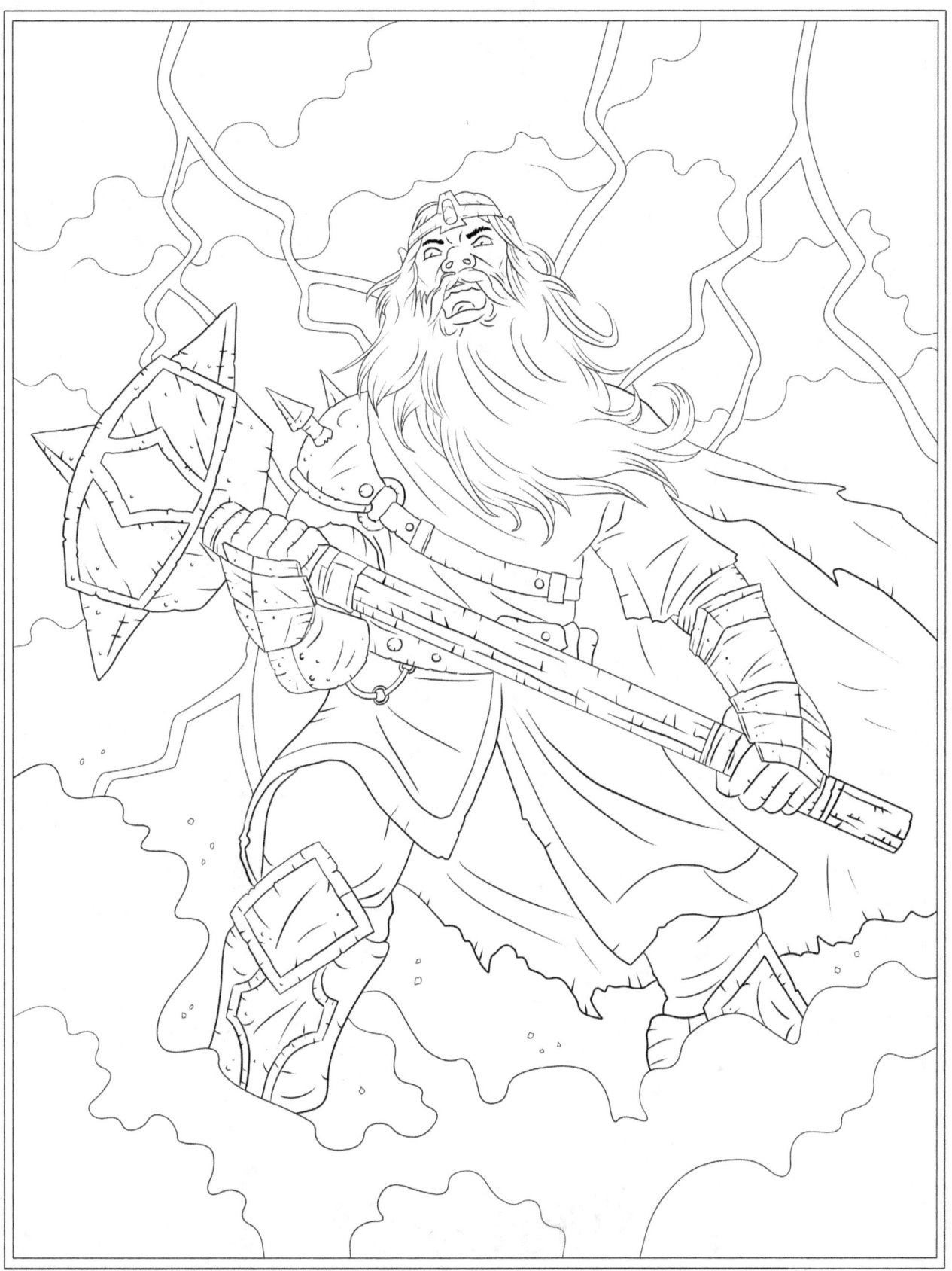

Elven Fighters

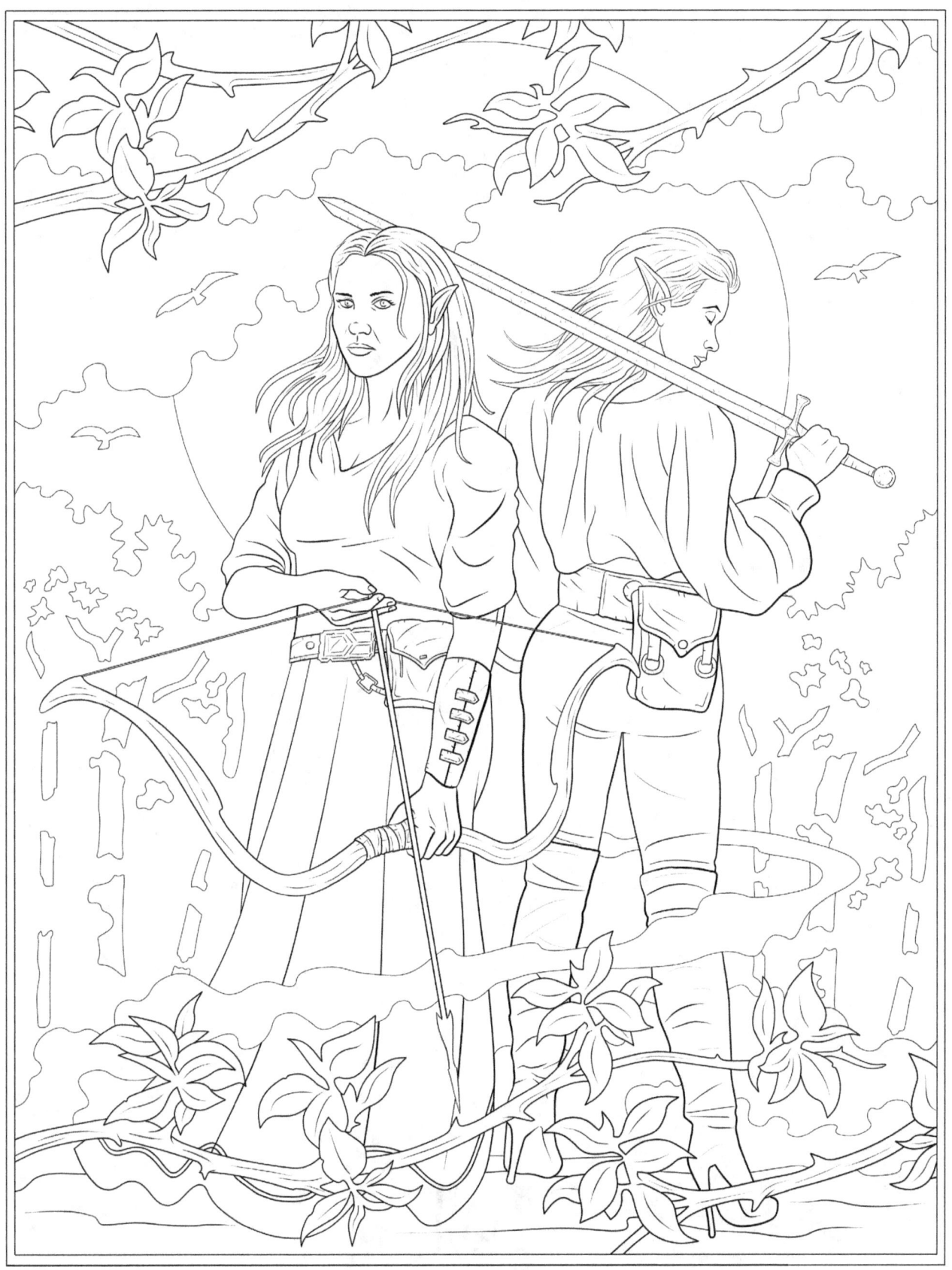

Troll

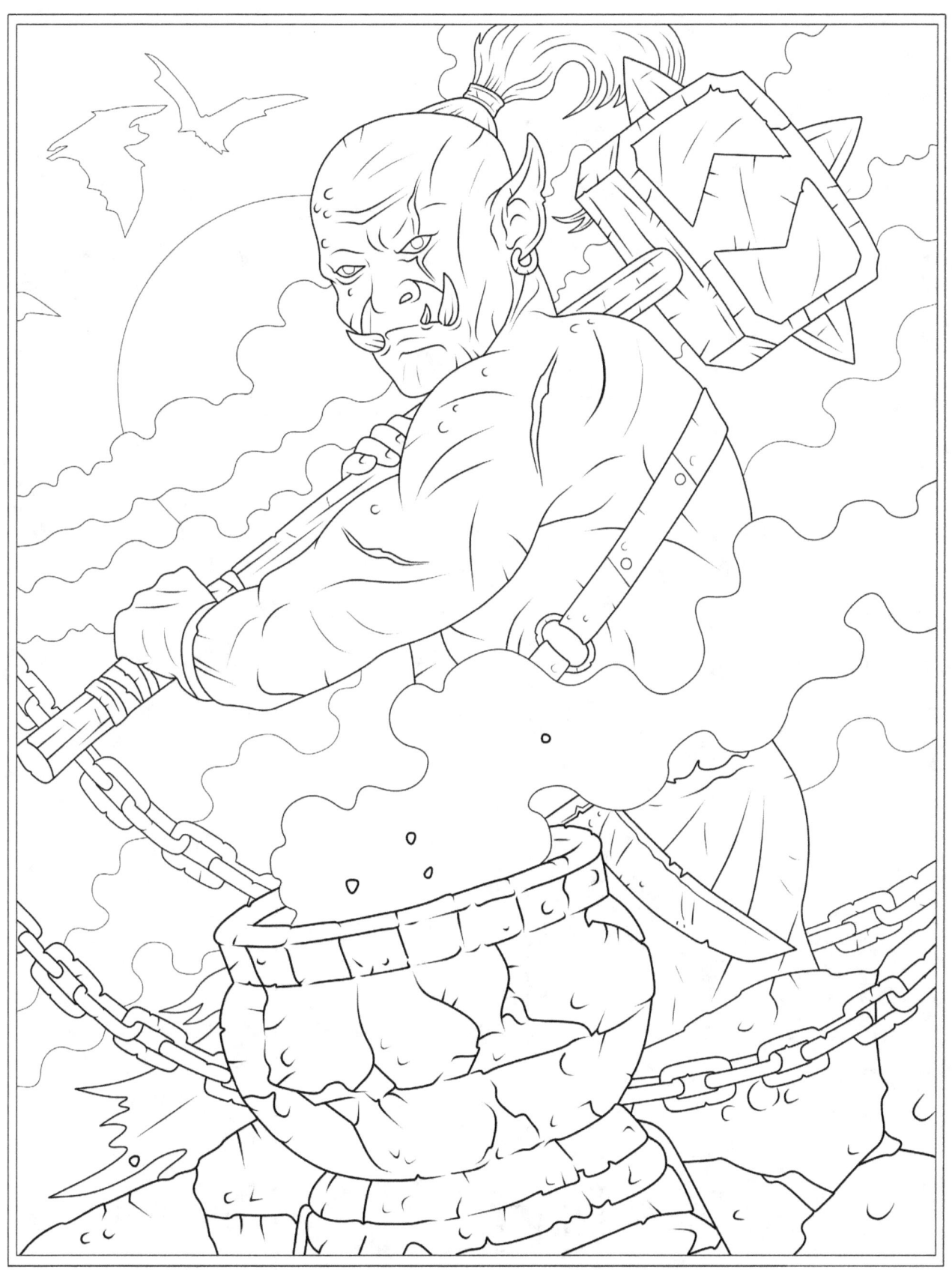

Water Sprite

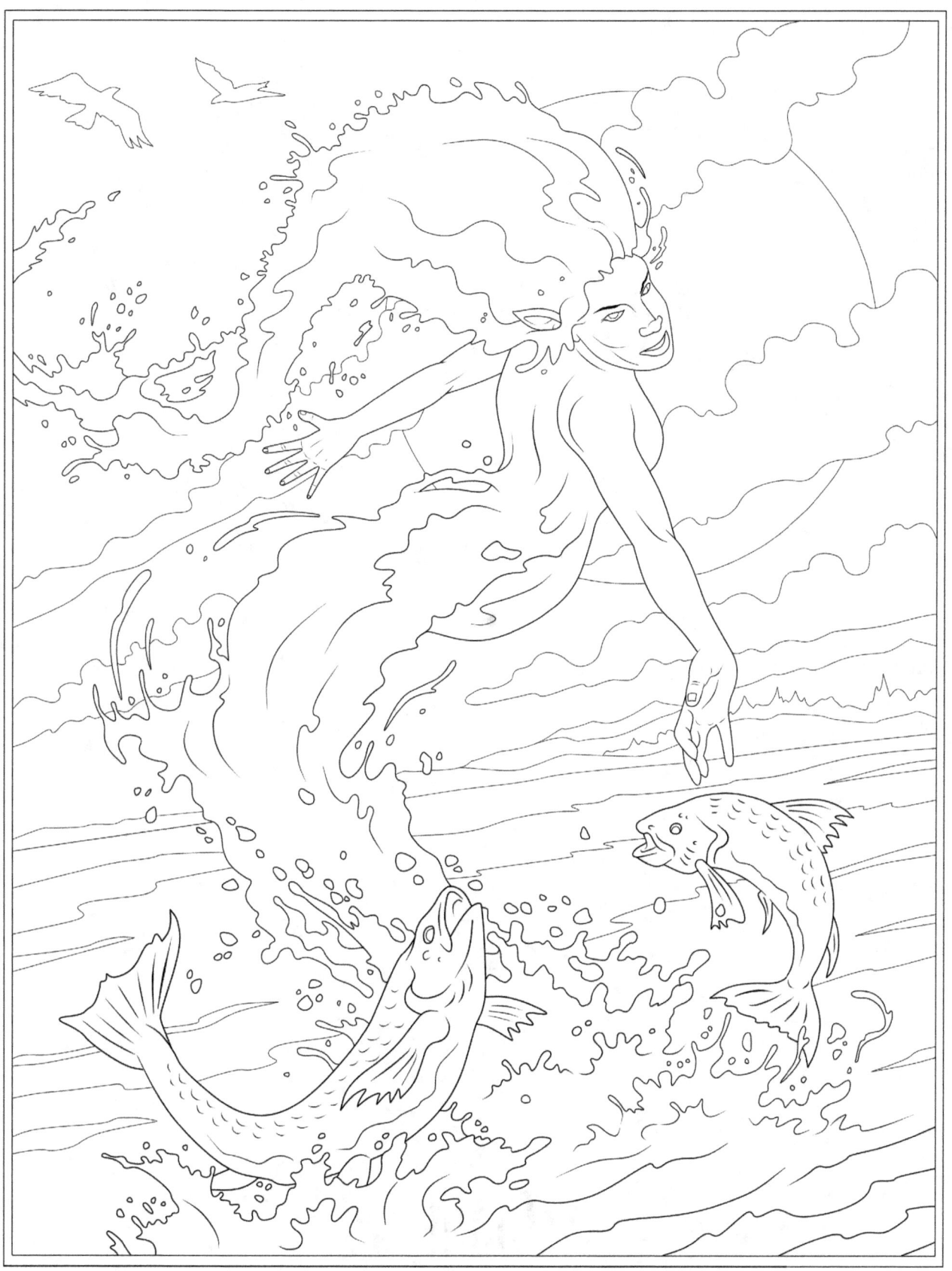

Giant

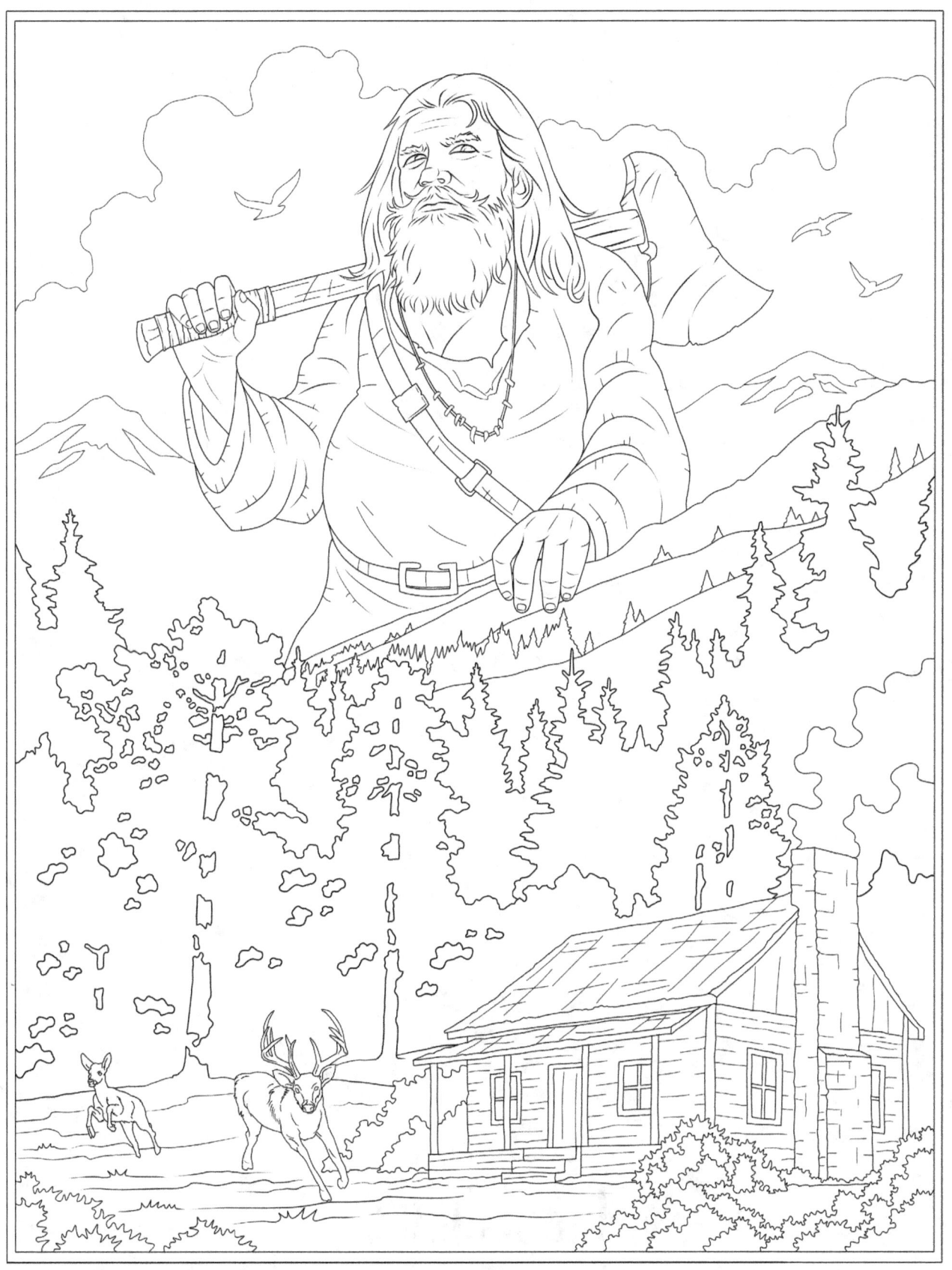

Giant Spider

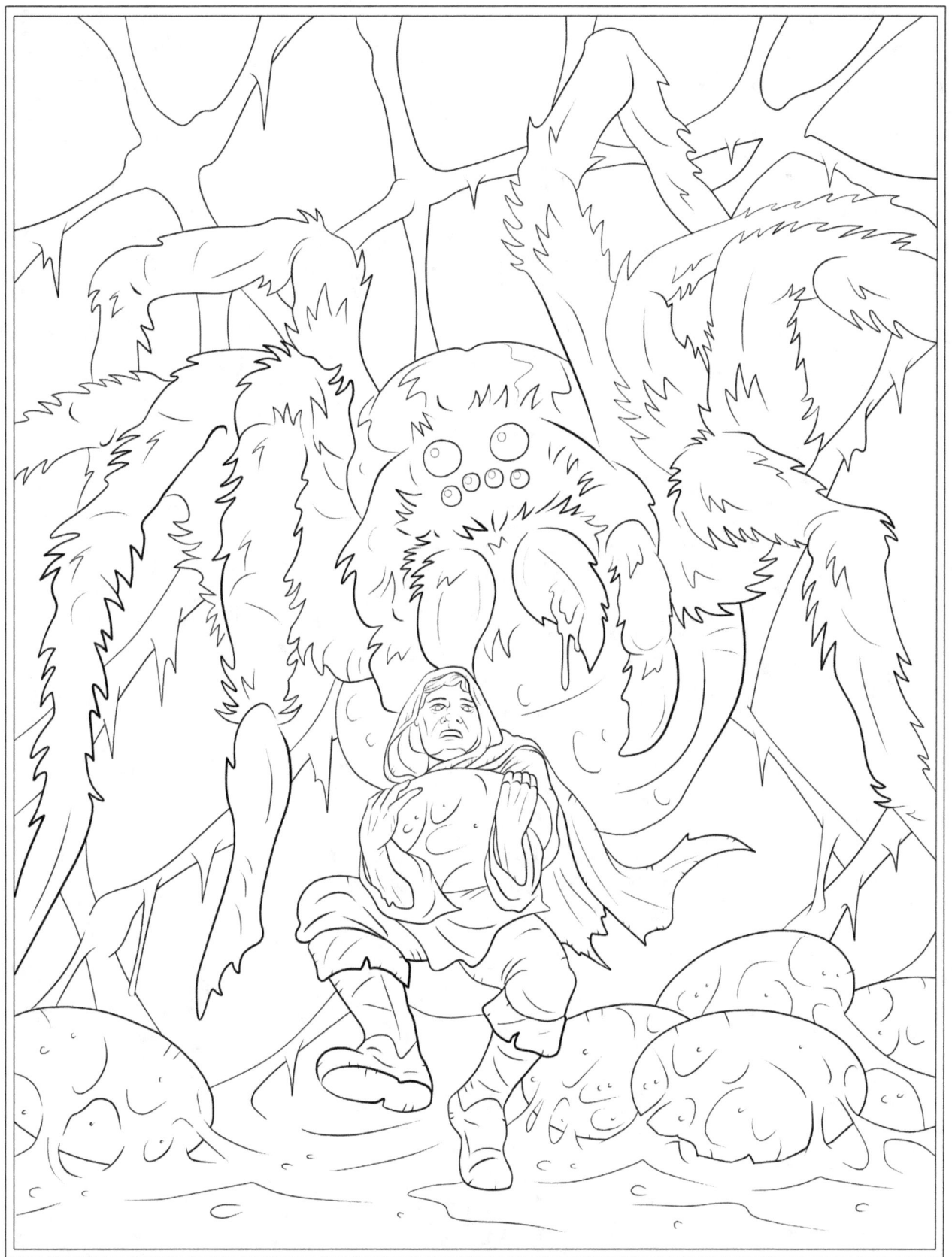

Faerie

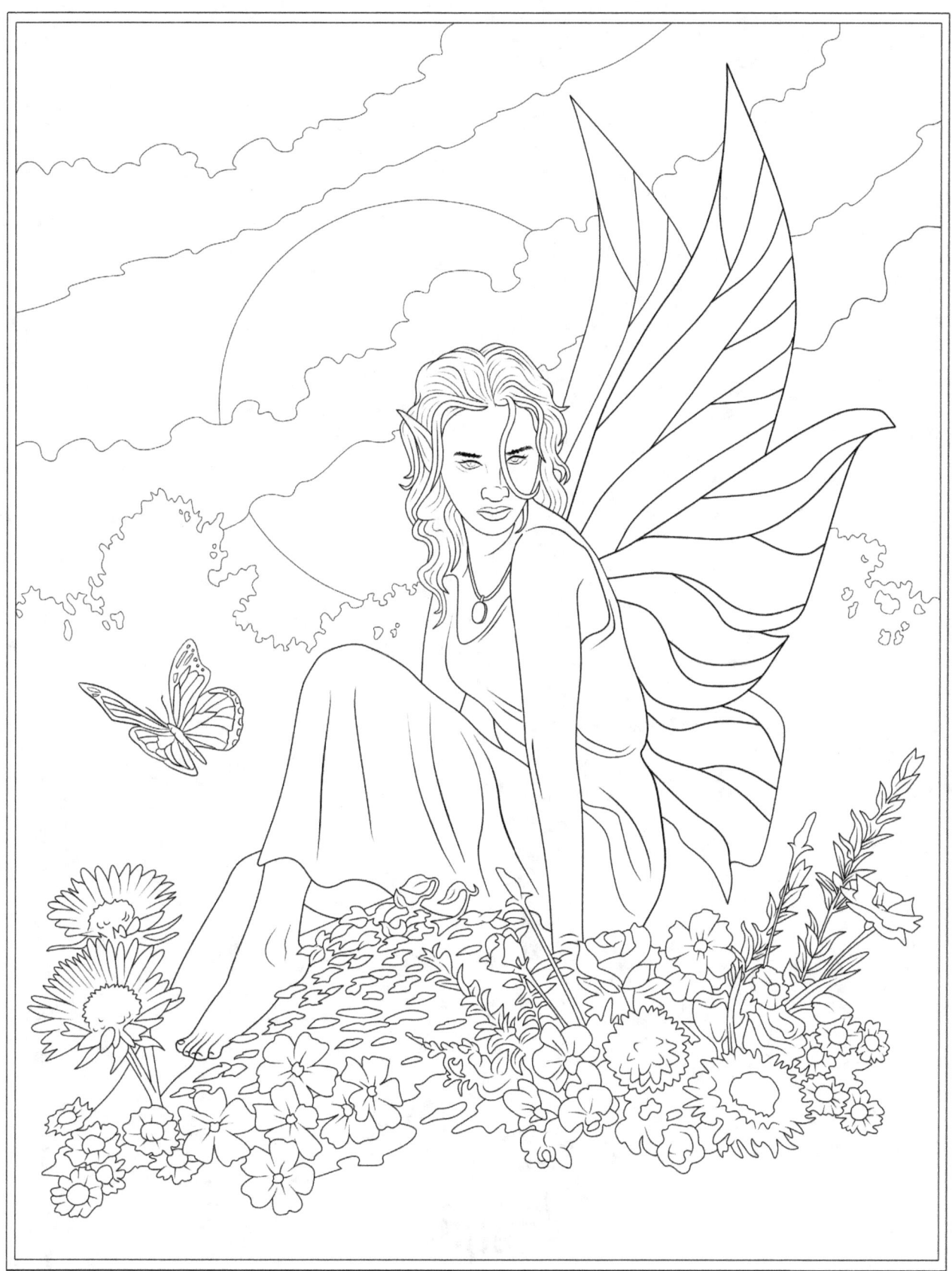

Vampire

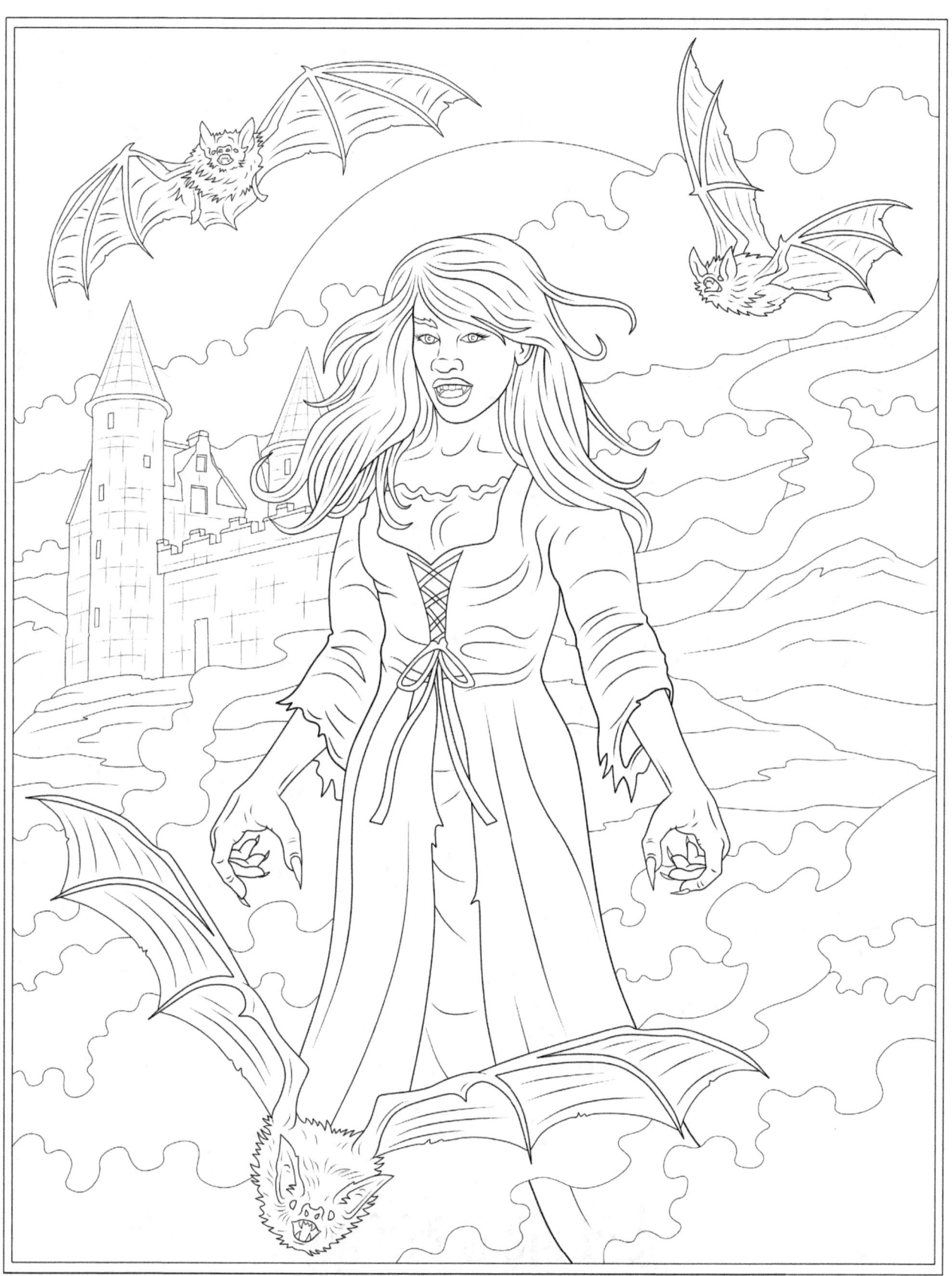

Gnome & Friend

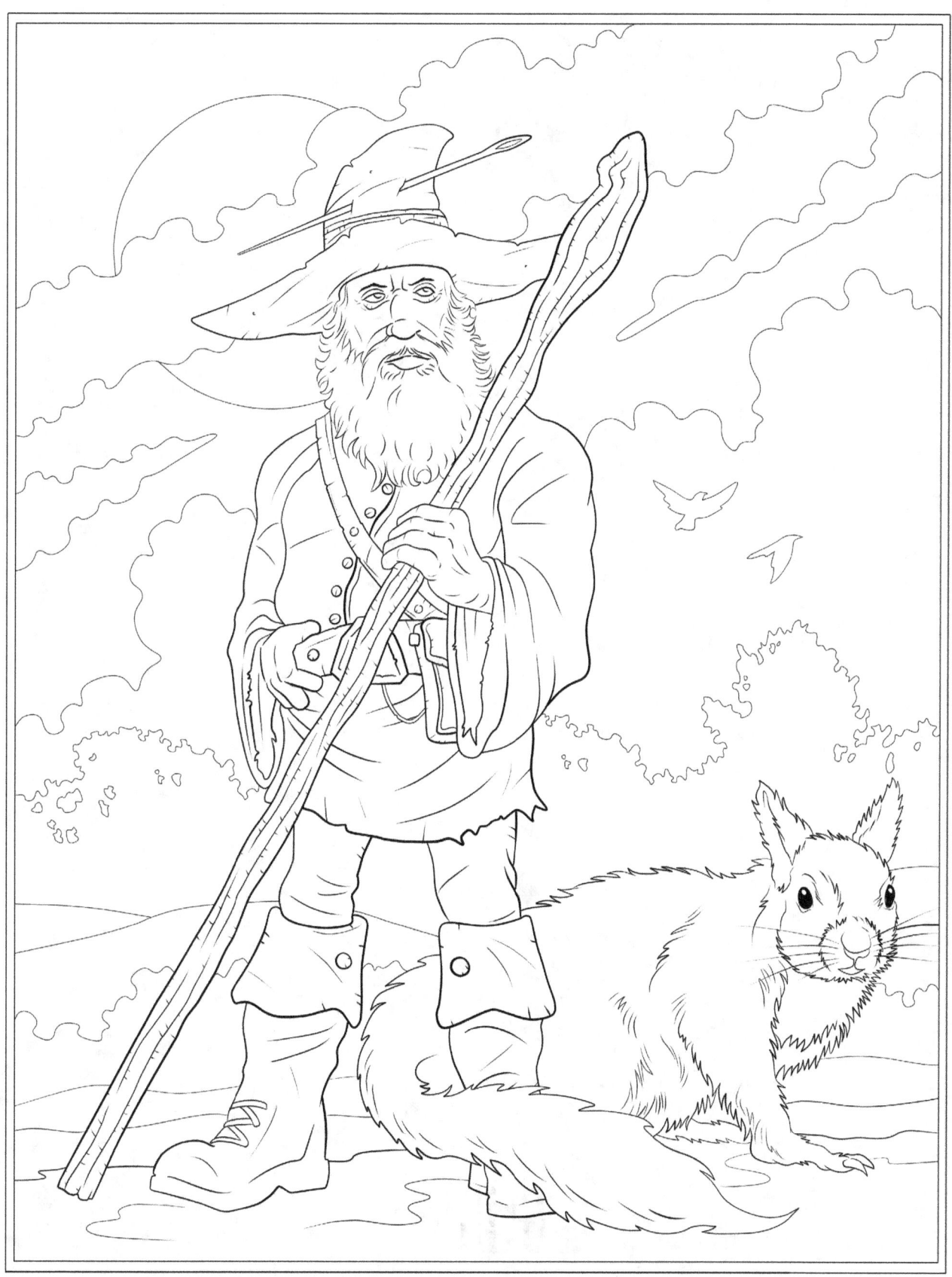

Griffin

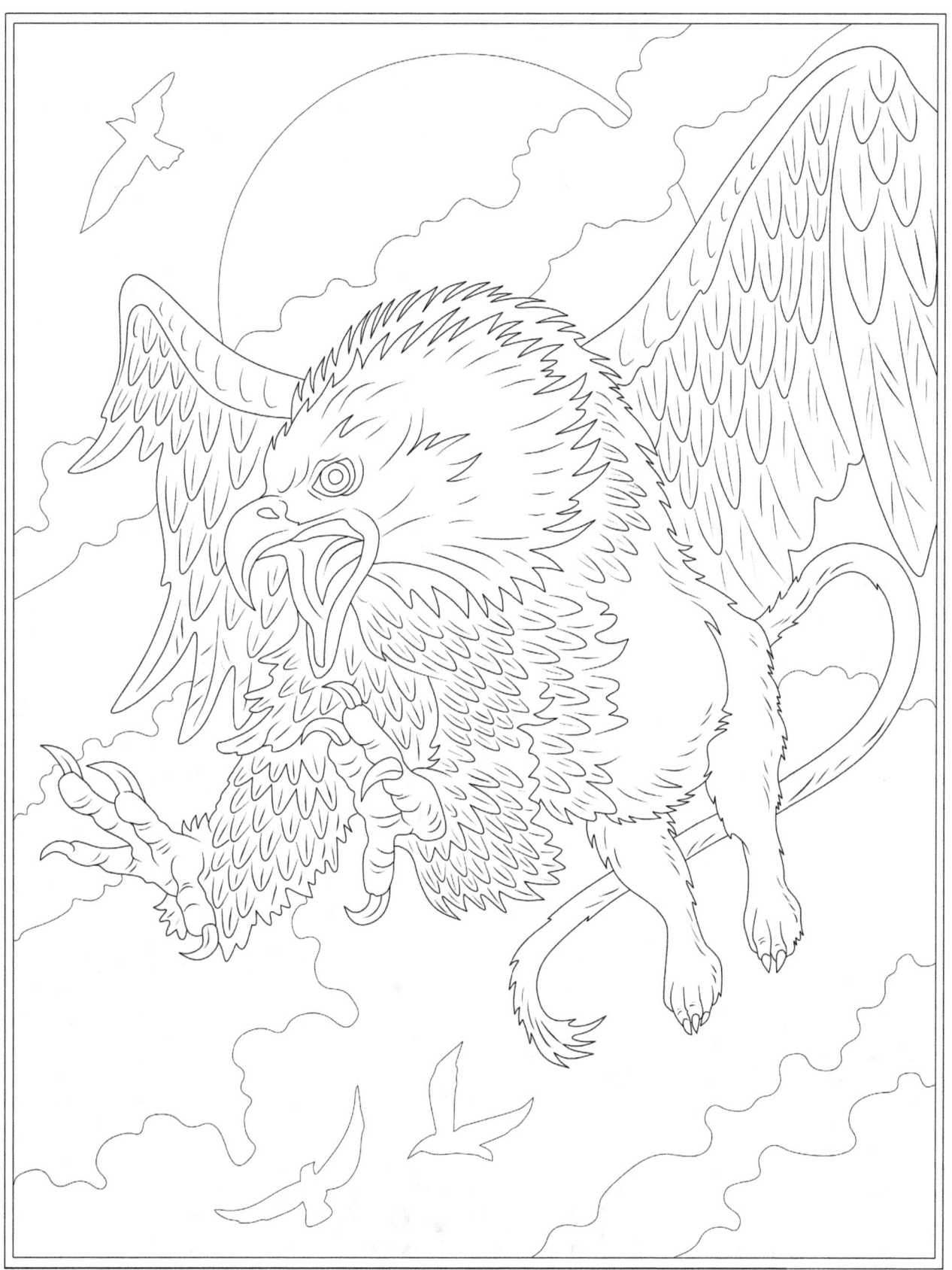

Undead Witch

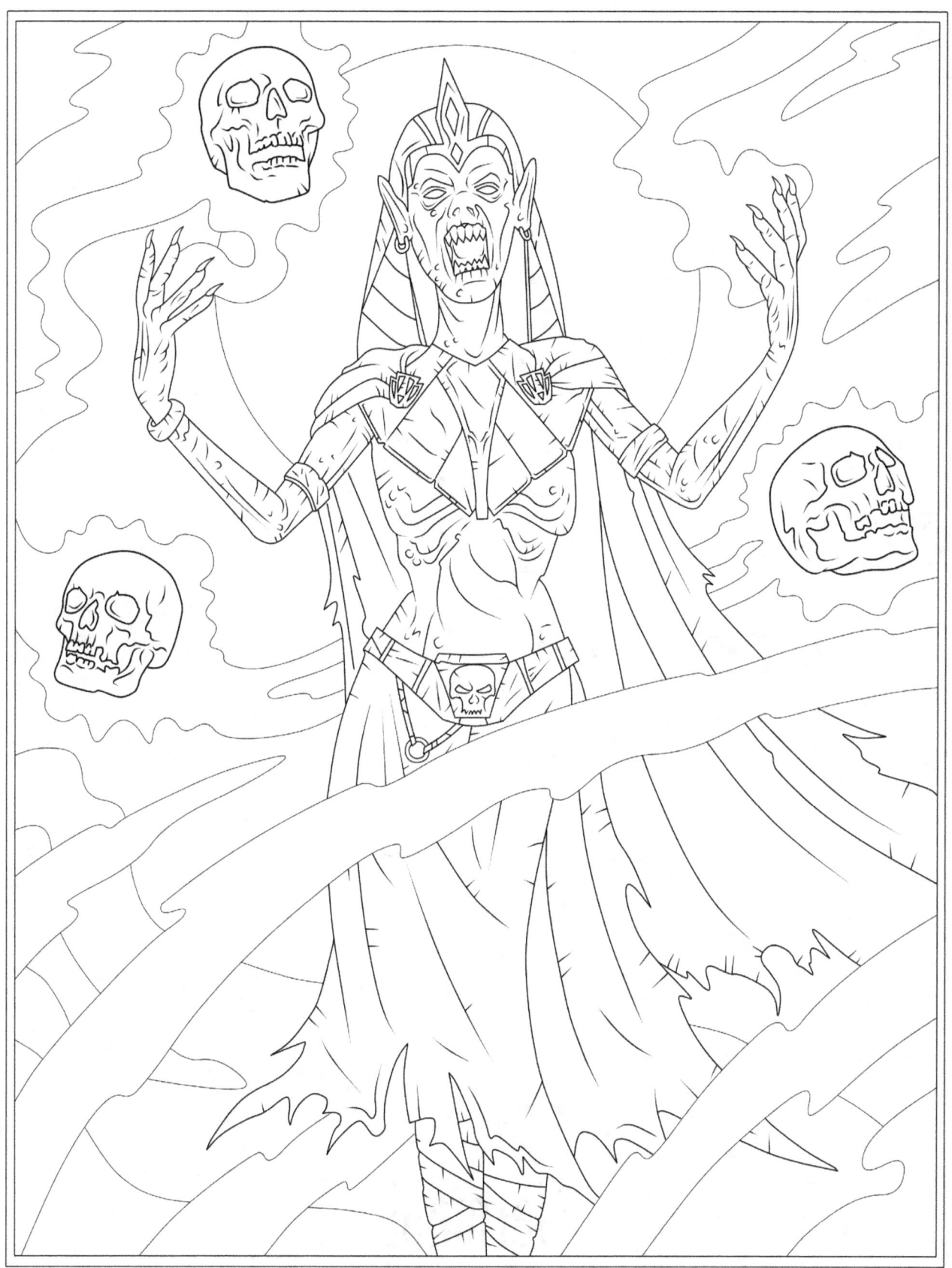

Mermaid

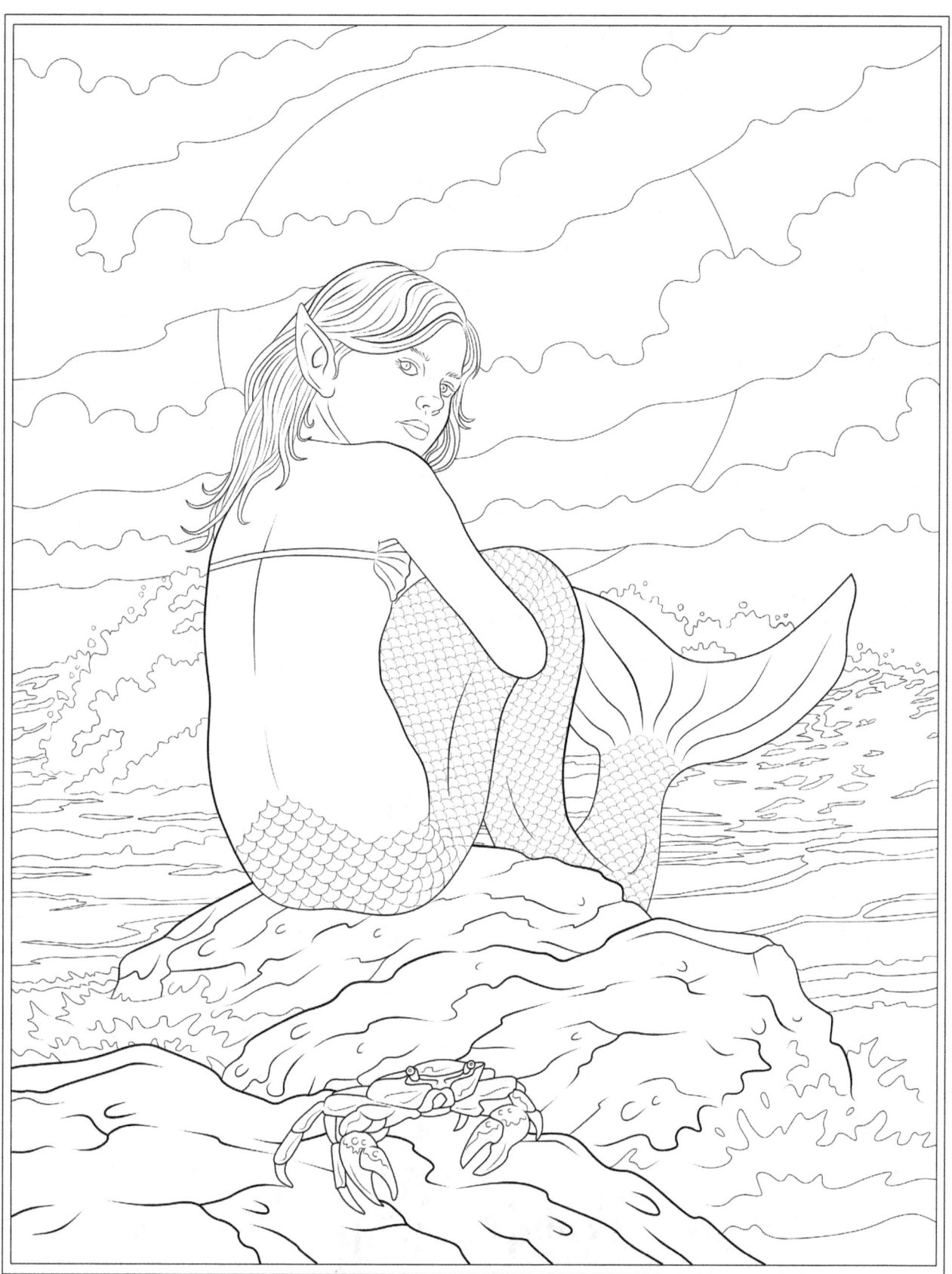

Skeleton Army

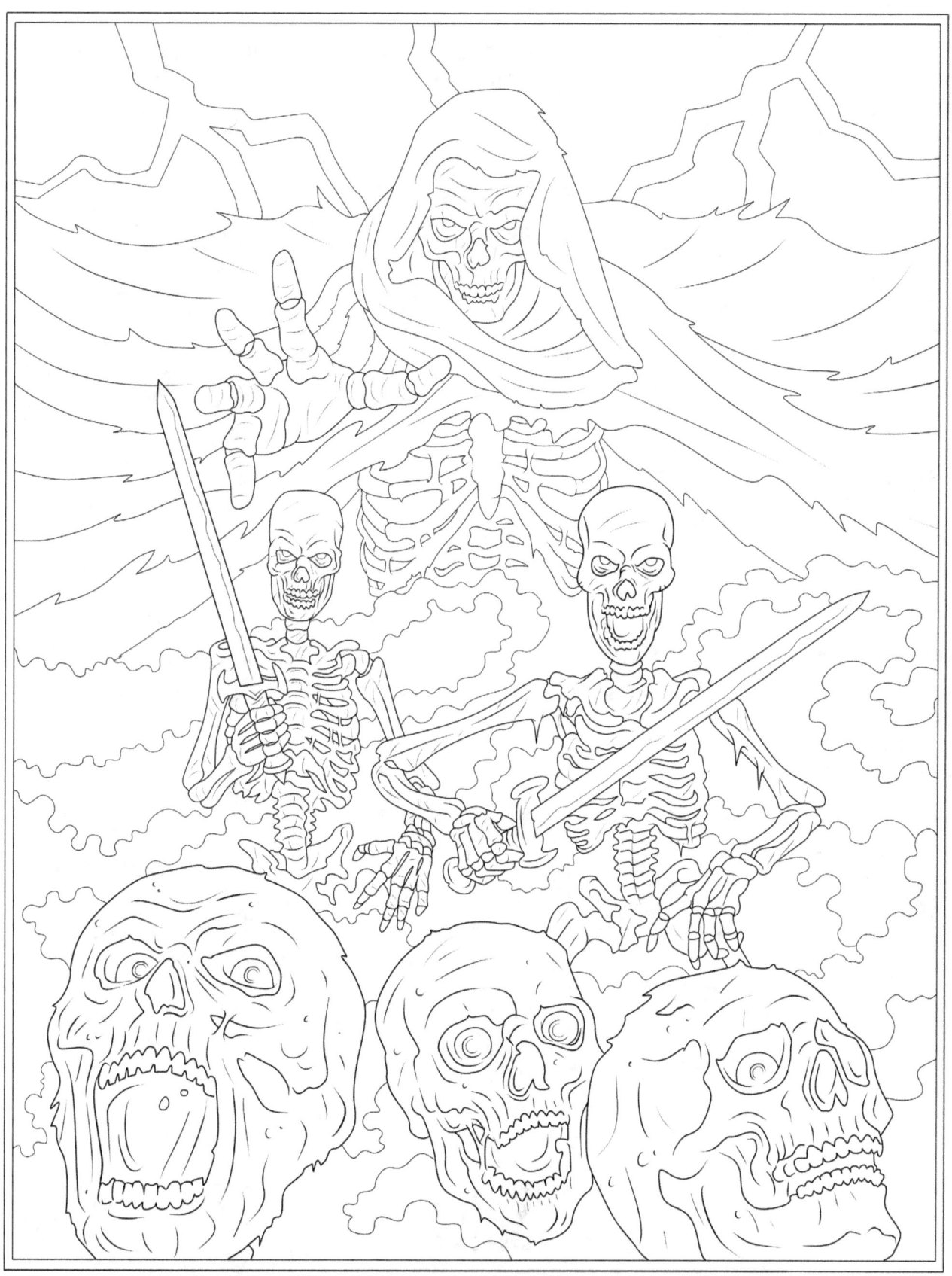

Satyr

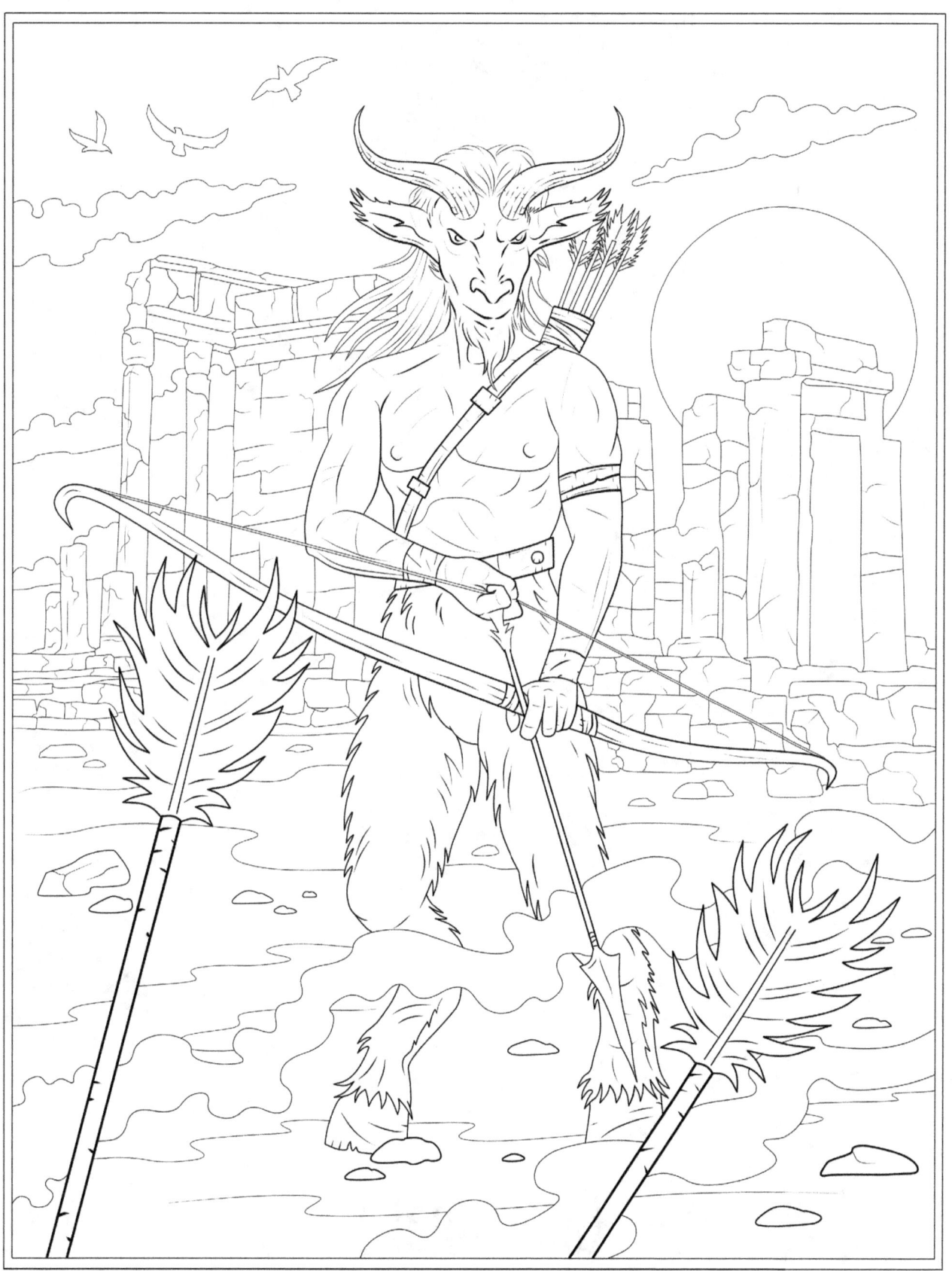

Giant Snake

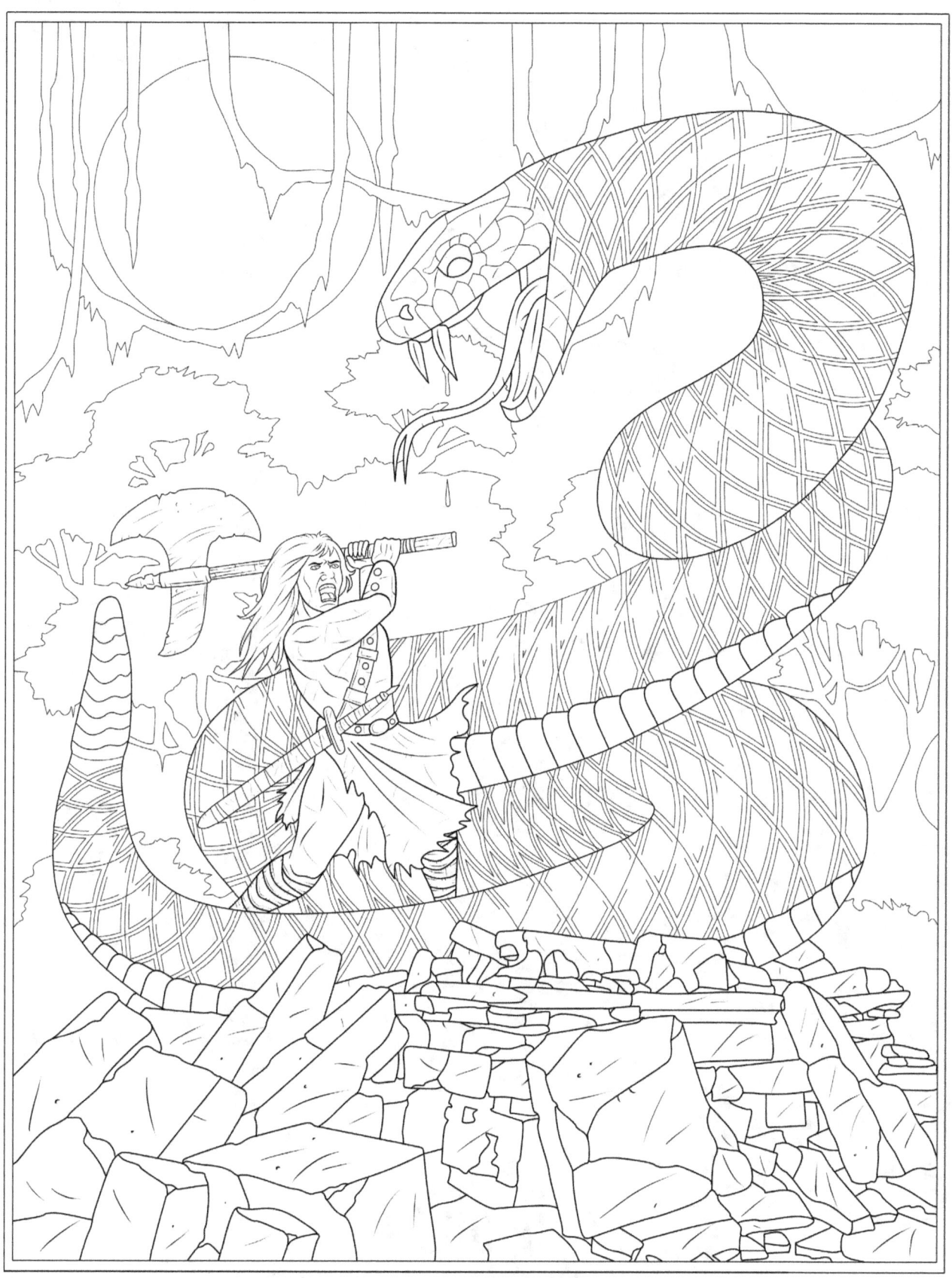

Goblin

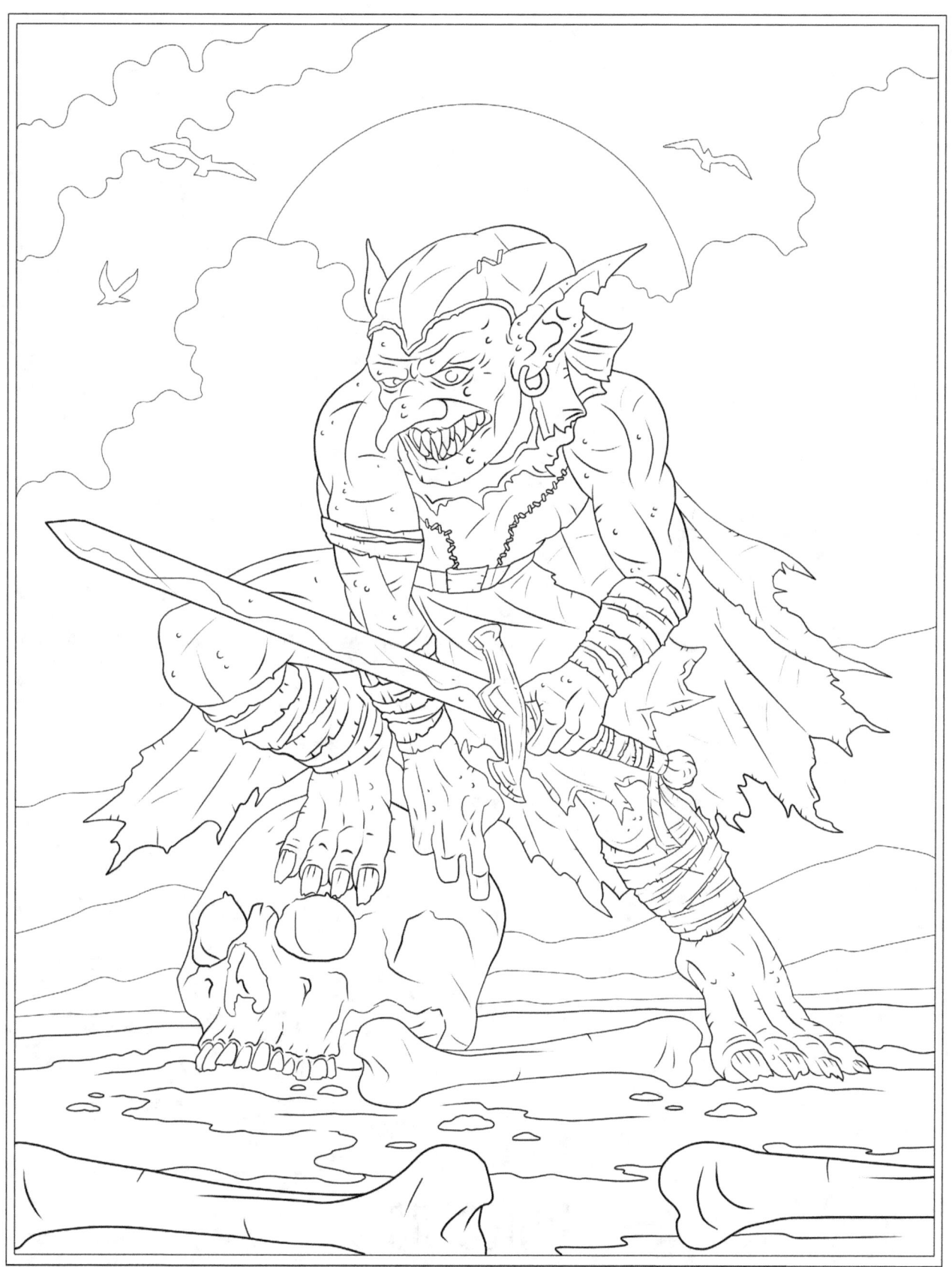

Unicorns

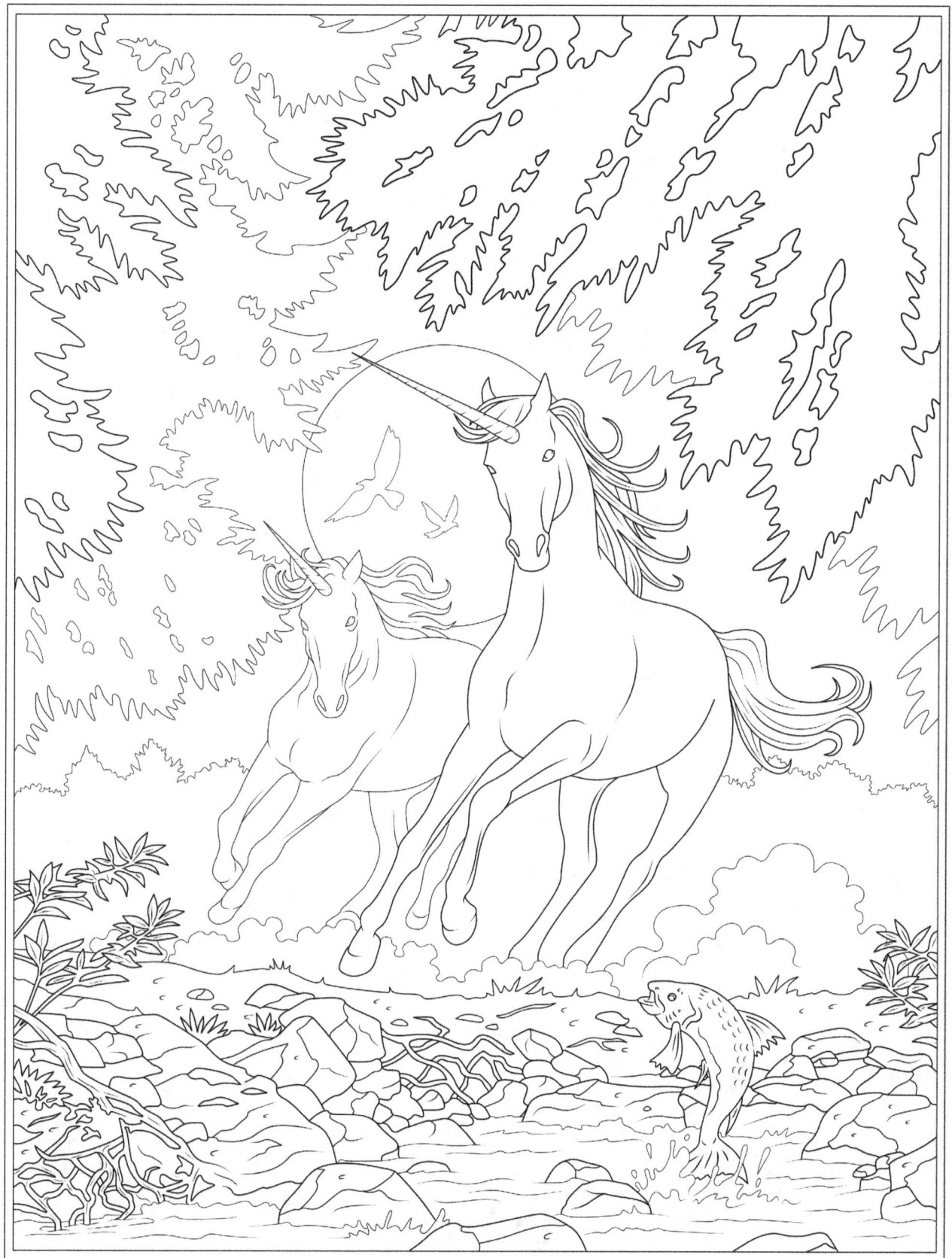

Minotaur

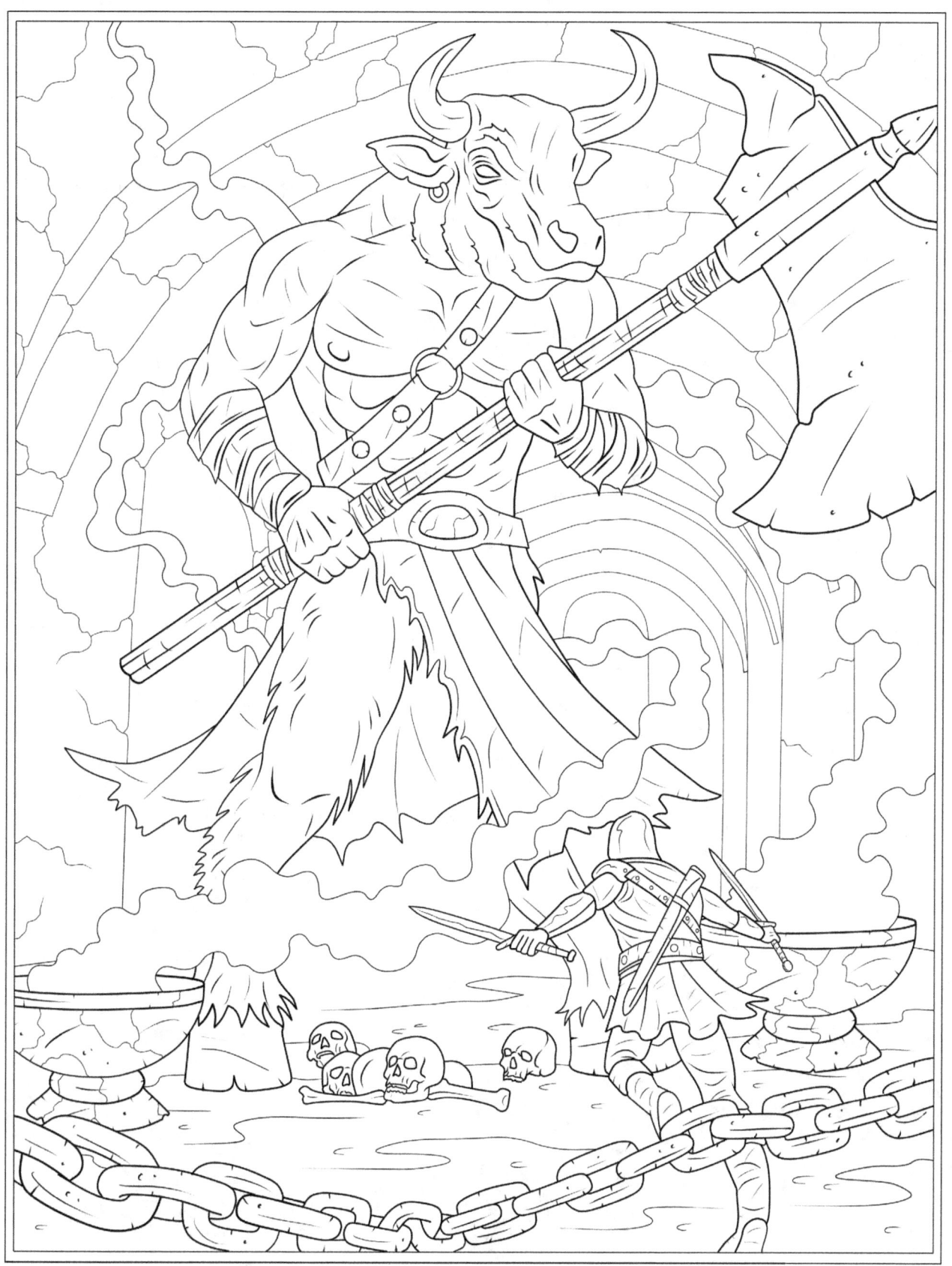

www.ingramcontent.com/pod-product-compliance
Lightning Source LLC
Chambersburg PA
CBHW081540220526
45467CB00010B/3277